HOW DOES A NETWORK WORK?

Matt Anniss

Published in paperback in 2016
First published in hardback in 2015
Copyright © Wayland 2015

Wayland
An imprint of
Hachette Children's Group
Part of Hodder & Stoughton
Carmelite House
50 Victoria Embankment
London EC4Y 0DZ

Produced for Wayland by Calcium
Design by Simon Borrough

Picture Acknowledgements:
Cover: Shutterstock: Dukes. Inside: Dreamstime: Ajv123ajv 35andresr
34andyb1126 12, Arekmalang 1, 18, Avava 8, Clearviewstock 24, Cpubrp 29,
Darrinhenry 39, Eldadcarin 33l, Elenathewise 31b, Ersler 37b, Flik47 15m,
Fotoplanner 15t, Georgios 25, Gtmedia 43, Guynamedjames 17, Icefields 19b,
Ilona75 45, Innershadows 26, Iofoto 30, Joegough 16, Jojojojo 22, Lucadp 9,
Markhunt 10, Monkeybusinessimages 5, Nruboc 4, Nyul 13, Rabbit75 11t,
Rafalolechowski 14, Reinhold68 32, Route66 44, Sebcz 20, Shanti 38, Stelya
27, Wavebreakmediamicro 40, Wksp 7, Xalanx 6; Shutterstock: Paulo Afonso
28, Ermolaev Alexander 19t, Asharkyu 11b, Dziurek 41, Robert Kneschke
36, Leungchopan 33r, Michaeljung 23, Mihai Simonia 21, Pavel L Photo and
Video 37t, YanLev 3, 31t; Wikimedia: Pete Souza 42.

A catalogue record for this book is available from the British Library

ISBN: 978 0 7502 9078 4
Library Ebook ISBN: 978 0 7502 9077 7

Printed in China
10 9 8 7 6 5 4 3 2 1

MIX
Paper from
responsible sources
FSC® C104740

An Hachette UK company
www.hachette.co.uk
www.hachettechildrens.co.uk

CONTENTS

CHAPTER ONE

WHAT IS A NETWORK?

Today, networks are all around us. They give us power, connect us to the world and provide us with entertainment. Thanks to networks, we can check e-mails on a smartphone, play games with people, watch live sports on television or on the Internet and be connected to friends at the touch of a button.

Talking on mobile phones would not be possible without modern communications network technology.

Using networks

We rely on networks to live our day-to-day lives. Keeping in touch with friends and family, whether by using mobile phones, e-mail, letters or the Internet, would not be possible without high-tech networks. We would not be able to buy the things we want using one click of a mouse, have groceries delivered or pay electricity bills over the phone. Without networks we would not even have 'old-fashioned' landline telephones in our homes or offices.

Thanks to computer network technology, we can record, pause, fast-forward and rewind cable and satellite television.

Networks made easy

The technology needed to create today's high-tech networks is very complicated, but the principles behind it are simple. Networks connect things, be they electrical power lines, telephone cables or computers. Networks have existed for many years but it is only in the last 200 years that they have revolutionised our lives. For example, hundreds of years ago, there were simple postal networks for sending and receiving letters. However, it was only in the 1900s that these networks became widespread and accessible enough for everyone to use.

Modern networks

This book is concerned with the cutting-edge technology of today's computer and entertainment networks. These are the systems that allow people to send and receive communications, such as e-mails and telephone calls and share information. You will find out how the Internet works, how it is possible to remotely connect computers around the world and how the 'information technology' age has changed the way we live our lives.

THE FIRST NETWORK

The first system to use electricity to transmit messages over huge distances was the electric telegraph. The first electric telegraph line opened in the United States between Washington D.C. and Baltimore in 1844. The electric telegraph allowed people to send messages in the form of words spelt out using short bursts of electrical noise. This system was called Morse code, after its inventor, Samuel Morse.

GET CONNECTED

We use many different networks in our everyday lives. Some connect us to electronic devices in our homes, while others help us communicate with the rest of the world. Before learning how computer networks work, it is important to learn about the many different types of network and what they do.

Even young children can now use high-tech network technology to access the Internet and print out pictures.

USB cables, like this one plugged into a laptop, allow you to connect a number of devices together to form a PAN.

Personal area network

The most basic network is the one that exists around us. This network is the connections that enable our personal electronic devices, such as computers, printers, smartphones and music players, to communicate with each other. For example, at home you may have a desktop computer that is connected to a printer or a musical keyboard, using a USB cable. The computer may also be connected to a modem, which in turn allows you to access the Internet. From time to time, you may also connect your smartphone to the computer to copy over music or movie clips. This simple network of electronic devices is known as a personal area network (PAN).

Cables or wireless

When you print a document or download photographs from a digital camera, you are using your PAN. Any electronic devices you plug into your computer using a cable are part of this personal network.

Instead of using traditional wires, devices in your PAN can also be connected using wireless technology, such as Bluetooth or WiFi. These use invisible radio waves used to send and receive information.

BLUETOOTH

Bluetooth is a wireless technology that allows electronic devices, such as smartphones and laptop computers, to share, send and receive information over very short distances — a few metres at best. The information, or data, is sent, received and shared between Bluetooth devices using invisible radio waves.

7

LOCAL AREA NETWORK

A PAN usually contains just one computer. If you wanted to connect a number of computers, you would need to set up a local area network (LAN).

LANs are used in schools and universities to allow students to connect to the Internet so that they can access coursework notes.

LAN power

There are millions of LANs all around the world. Some, such as those used by schools, universities and businesses, connect a large number of computers in the same building. This enables these computers to share resources, information and access to the Internet. However, LANs need not be this big. If you have two or more computers in your home and they share a single Internet connection, then you are using a simple LAN.

Ethernet revolution

At home, your LAN may be wirelessly connected using WiFi technology. However, for a large LAN with several computers, such as a LAN in a library or office building, the computers will be connected using wires called Ethernet cables. One of the main tasks of most LANs is allowing people to share computer files. Many large LANs do this by using a central storage computer, called a server. All the computers in the network will be connected to the server (see pages 18–19).

USING ETHERNET CABLES

Ethernet cables were invented in 1980 to allow speedy connections between several computers in a LAN. The cables work by breaking large amounts of data into tiny 'virtual packets' called frames. These frames can then be sent from one computer to another in the same LAN in just a fraction of a second.

LAN parties

Some people use their LAN to play games with their friends. For many years, PC gaming enthusiasts have hosted 'LAN parties', with up to 20 people playing against each other, over one local area network, in a large room or garage.

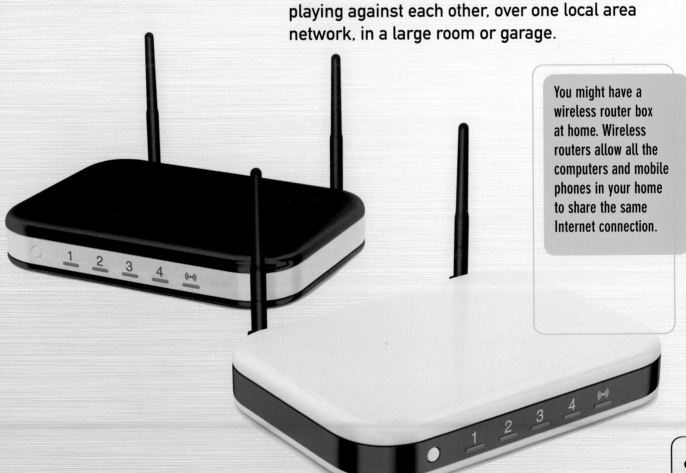

You might have a wireless router box at home. Wireless routers allow all the computers and mobile phones in your home to share the same Internet connection.

METROPOLITAN AREA NETWORK

LANs connect computers in a small area, usually inside the same building. A network that connects a number of different LANs over a larger area is called a metropolitan area network (MAN).

Just the right size

According to the Institute of Electrical and Electronics Engineers (IEEE), the organisation that decides on worldwide communications standards, a metropolitan network can vary in size from a few blocks or a cluster of buildings to an entire city. The largest MANs can be up to 70 square kilometres (30 square miles) large. However, most MANs are much smaller than this and are roughly the size of a large university campus.

Businesses rely on MANs to connect people working in different office buildings in one town or city.

Joined together by underground cables, the LANs in all of these buildings make up a MAN.

Gateway to the world

Many businesses and large organisations, such as local councils and police forces, use MANs to securely connect LANs in different buildings and locations. This means that instead of connecting fewer than 100 computers, they can potentially connect thousands. The main point of MANs is to connect small LANs to what is known as the wide area network (WAN) – the worldwide network of cables that carries computer communications around the world. MANs are our gateway to the World Wide Web.

FIBRE OPTIC CABLES

Today, most computer communications between LANs and MANs are carried along special fibre optic cables. These cables turn computer data into pulses of light, which can travel down the fibre optic cables at incredibly fast speeds. At the other end of the cable, the pulses of light are then turned back into data that the computer can understand.

Modern fibre optical cables can contain up to 1,000 fibres in a single cable.

WIDE AREA NETWORK

The WAN is the system of fibre optic cables, telephone cables and communication satellites that connects every country on Earth. It is what allows us to phone friends abroad, check e-mails, surf the Internet on our smartphones and play computer games against people in other countries.

WHAT EXACTLY IS THE WAN?

The WAN is a global series of smaller (but still enormous) connected networks. Some of these networks are the size of whole countries, while others are as big as entire regions. Together, these networks connect everyone to the wider world.

The WAN is what allows people to keep in contact with friends and family around the world on social networking sites, such as Facebook.

Transport for data

The WAN is like a kind of communications transport system. Just as motorways, train lines and aeroplane routes allow us to travel around the country and the world, the cables and satellites of the WAN allow telephone calls, television shows and computer data to do the same.

Using the same transport example, your local MAN is like the bus or train services that allow you to move freely around your hometown or city. However, to go further afield, you need to connect to the WAN.

WAN size fits all

Every time you connect to the Internet or you use a computer to send an e-mail to someone, you are connecting to the WAN. You connect to the WAN through the other three networks – PAN, LAN and MAN. Connecting to the WAN is done in just millionths of a second, without you even noticing.

People use the WAN for many things, including playing computer games against people in other cities or countries.

CHAPTER TWO

HOW NETWORKS WORK

We have seen how the different types of high-tech network allow us to connect to, and communicate with, the world around us. How do these networks really work? Data, in the form of electrical signals, light or sound, is transported around the world using fixed cables or through the air via radio waves.

This is a close-up of the inside of a server, which is used to store and direct information across a network.

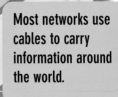

Most networks use cables to carry information around the world.

Cables and radio waves

For a network to function properly, it must decide whether to connect using cables or wirelessly, using radio waves. Some networks use just one method, while others use a combination of the two. Both do the same thing in different ways. Systems that use cables turn data, sound or pictures into electrical signals (or, as in the case of fibre optic cables: light), which then travel down wires to their destination. At the other end, the signals are then turned back into data, sound or pictures. This is the system used by landline telephone networks, cable television and most computer networks.

Satellite television is one of many networks that use radio waves to send and receive information through the air.

Through the air

Today, more networks use radio waves to transmit the same information over long distances. This is how mobile phone networks operate, how satellite television works and how we can connect wirelessly to the Internet using WiFi. Radio waves are invisible waves of energy that can travel enormous distances. However, radio waves are not as reliable at sending data as cables, which is why mobile phone calls sometimes break up and the picture on satellite television services looks grainy during periods of bad weather.

CAN RADIO WAVES FAIL?

Radio waves do not actually fail but because they are sent through the air, they can be affected by the weather and other services that use similar technology. Different types of network use different lengths of radio wave to transmit information. Radio waves that only have to travel short distances are less likely to fail.

CLIENT AND HOST

Every second of each day, huge amounts of information flow through the cables and wireless services that power our networks. This information takes the form of hundreds of millions of individual requests. These requests could be to fulfill a task, such as sending an e-mail or for specific information, such as carrying out an Internet search on a search engine such as Google.

Network access

The different requests flow between 'clients' and 'hosts'. The client is the person using a particular piece of technology to access the network. For example, this device could be a laptop computer or a smartphone. The host can be either the place where the information is stored, such as the computer that stores a particular website, or the company that provides the service, such as a mobile phone network provider or the Internet service provider.

This mobile phone transmitter acts as a host, sending and receiving information to and from the clients, which are the mobile phones.

All around us

In our day-to-day lives, we make a huge number of client-host requests. Every time we make a phone call, watch a video on websites such as YouTube, post things to social media sites such as Facebook or download an MP3 file, we are requesting and receiving, information from a host.

It does not stop there. When you switch on a light at home, you are making a request to the electrical power network. It is the same if we switch on a gas cooker or buy a ticket for a trip. Client and host interactions are all around us.

SUPER-SIZE HOST

One of the world's most popular search engines, Google, requires a huge number of super-size host computers, called servers, to handle the number of Internet search requests it receives every day. Although the information is classified, some experts believe that Google uses more than 2 million servers to power its online services.

When you access Google Maps on your phone, you are acting as a client, requesting a service from a host (in this case Google).

SERVERS

Servers are the huge, incredibly powerful computers that act as hosts. They handle hundreds of millions of individual network requests every day. Without these super-computers, most of the networks on which we rely would not work.

Banks of servers connected with cables are a common sight in many office buildings and universities.

Powerful hosts

Servers are not like normal computers. As well as being hundreds of times more powerful than an average home computer, they are usually designed to do one specific task. This could be storing Web pages or media, such as the video clips on YouTube and the music files we download, or performing a specific task, such as allowing us to send and receive e-mails. Every time you connect to the Internet, you access servers. When you send an e-mail to a friend, your computer will make a connection to your Internet service provider's mail server. Before your friend receives the e-mail, he or she will have to access the service provider's mail server to download the message.

Servers at school

Servers are also used in much smaller networks, such as the LANs used in schools or offices. Here, the server is usually used as a place to store documents that can be accessed by many different computer users at the same time. These could include coursework notes, company accounts or important paperwork.

School servers can store information so that learners can access it while doing their coursework.

BACK-UP SERVERS

Servers are so important to large Internet companies such as Apple, Amazon and Google that their systems include a huge number of back-up servers. This means that if they receive more requests at the same time than their regular servers can handle, additional requests will be rerouted to the back-up servers.

The banks of servers used by companies such as Google can hold more information in them than all of the books in this library.

HUBS AND ROUTERS

With billions of network requests every day, it is important for those who run networks to put in place technology that helps information flow freely. In today's computer networks, this is done using hubs, switches and routers.

YouTube uses switches to ensure its website never crashes as a result of too many people requesting to watch videos.

Hubs

A network hub is a box into which you can plug a number of network devices, such as computers and printers. The devices are linked to the hub using Ethernet cables (see page 9). In a school, office, or university campus, the network hub links together the devices in a LAN. Usually, it will also allow each of these computers to access a single, shared link to the Internet.

Switches

Network switches are used to ensure that requests reach their intended target. This could be a particular computer, Web service or Internet server. Large Internet companies, such as Amazon and Google, also use switches to manage the amount of requests they receive. If a particular server gets more requests than it can handle, the network switch will push the request to a back-up server.

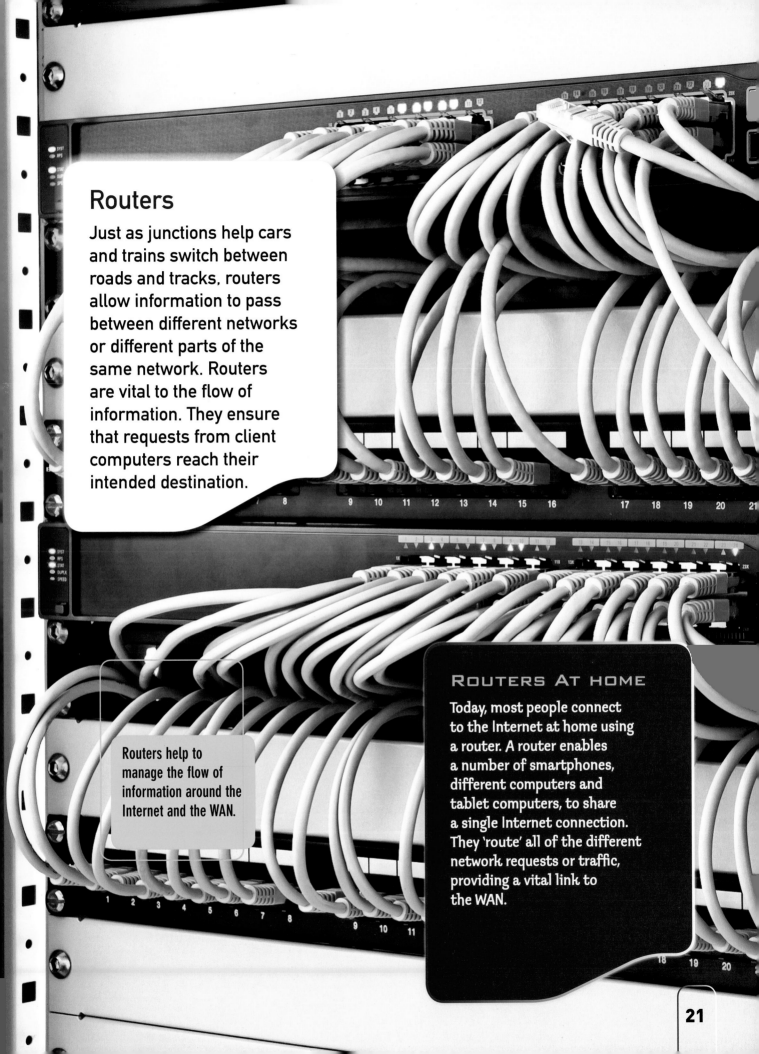

Routers

Just as junctions help cars and trains switch between roads and tracks, routers allow information to pass between different networks or different parts of the same network. Routers are vital to the flow of information. They ensure that requests from client computers reach their intended destination.

Routers help to manage the flow of information around the Internet and the WAN.

ROUTERS AT HOME

Today, most people connect to the Internet at home using a router. A router enables a number of smartphones, different computers and tablet computers, to share a single Internet connection. They 'route' all of the different network requests or traffic, providing a vital link to the WAN.

LAYERS AND PROTOCOLS

We now know how information moves around networks and the different technology used to make it happen. So how is the data organised as it flows around the world?

Rules of the Internet

In order for computers to communicate and for information to reach its intended target, networks use a set of rules. These rules are known as protocols. Protocols establish how information passes through the Internet. Without protocols, you would have difficulty reading a particular website or even accessing well-known websites such as Wikipedia or Amazon.

Sending an e-mail may look simple, but your computer actually breaks it down into many smaller processes, all in a fraction of a second.

Even doing simple things on the Internet, such as surfing the Web or reading an e-mail, require many smaller processes called protocols.

Specific protocols

Each protocol allows us to do a different task. For example, a hypertext transfer protocol (HTTP) allows us to read websites. Transfer control protocol (TCP) and Internet Protocol (IP) ensure that we can connect to the correct host server to retrieve information or send and receive e-mails.

Protocol layers

Even simple tasks, such as surfing the Internet, require your computer to follow a number of protocols at the same time. Because of this, protocols are usually stacked up in layers. Just as it may take more than one filling to make a sandwich, it can take many layers of protocol to perform one network request.

THE MAGNIFICENT SEVEN

According to computer scientists, most networks use seven layers of protocol to send and receive information. The definition of each of these layers is incredibly complicated. Each layer is concerned with a specific part of the process, from the cables carrying the information to how it is displayed on your computer screen.

CHAPTER THREE: NETWORKS THROUGH TIME

Modern communications networks are incredibly complicated and capable of sending and receiving huge amounts of information. Yet it has not always been this way. Little more than 150 years ago, it was impossible to speak to someone in a neighbouring town without travelling to see them. So how did the current network-communication age come about?

In the past, telephone operators had to manually connect calls by plugging wires into holes at a telephone exchange like this one.

Telephone networks

In 1876, a Scottish scientist named Alexander Graham Bell filed patent papers for an invention that allowed two people in different places to talk to each other. Bell realised that, using a capable device, it was possible to send and receive sound using electrical wires. The telephone, as the device became known, was a revolutionary idea. Over the next 100 years, a network of cables carrying telephone lines began popping up all around the world, connecting people in different towns and countries. These connections were made possible by the cables themselves and by telephone exchanges.

Primitive routers

Telephone exchanges worked on the same principle that is used by today's network routers. For example, if you were to call someone who lived on the other side of the world, the electrical signal sent by your telephone would pass along a series of cables to a local exchange. At the local exchange, it would be diverted to an international exchange to begin its journey across oceans and continents. National and local exchanges at the other end of the line then push the signal towards its intended destination.

Today's high-tech networks would not be possible without the work of Alexander Graham Bell.

HOW DOES IT WORK?

When you speak into the mouthpiece of your telephone, your words are turned into electrical signals. These signals travel down electrical wires until they reach the telephone of the person you are calling. Here they are turned back into sound. All of this happens in a matter of milliseconds.

RADIO AND TELEVISION NETWORKS

Following the development of early telephone networks, it was not long before scientists discovered that it was possible to transmit sound through the air using radio waves. It was a discovery that paved the way for an entertainment revolution.

The portable radio, which could pick up radio shows broadcast hundreds of kilometres away, was one of the great inventions of the twentieth century.

Radio revolution

The principle behind radio is similar to that of telephone systems. Like the telephone, radio uses a transmitter and a receiver. The transmitter converts sound into electrical signals that can be broadcast as radio waves. The receiver picks up the signals and converts them back into sound. At first, scientists struggled to get radio waves to travel more than a few kilometres, but eventually they built larger, more powerful transmitters that could broadcast over thousands of kilometres.

Travelling pictures

Soon scientists realised that moving pictures could be sent through the air in a similar way. Like radio, the pictures and sound could be broken up into electrical signals for transmission. The receiver, in this case a television set, then turns these electrical signals back into sound and pictures. Television was even more revolutionary than radio. Networks of television transmitters were built to relay television signals around the world. These are the television equivalent of Internet routers or telephone exchanges.

Thanks to modern satellite technology, television news programmes can feature live reports from the place where the news is happening.

COMPUTER NETWORKS

Ever since the first computers were built by scientists in the 1950s and 1960s, the race was on to connect computers. It took nearly 50 years for international computer connections to become commonplace.

The Internet revolution

Early computers were very large and extremely expensive. Only governments, universities (most of whom built their own) and large international companies could afford them. Despite this, the world's few computer users were determined to link them together so that they could share information. In 1962, computer scientists at US telephone company AT&T built the world's first modem. It was capable of sending computer data using ordinary telephone lines. Establishing a connection between two modems was done in a similar way to making a phone call. The user had to dial the number of the modem with which they wished to communicate. The modem would later drive the Internet revolution.

One of the world's first networks allowed people all over the United States to buy tickets for American Airlines flights.

THE FIRST E-MAIL

In 1971, a US computer science researcher named Ray Tomlinson sent a short message, made up of just a few random letters, over the ARPANET network. At the time, the network was used by the US military. This message would go down in history as the world's first ever e-mail.

Giant leaps forward

In the years that followed, a number of cutting-edge developments pushed the boundaries of computer networks. In 1964, the US company IBM built the world's first telephone ticket reservation system for American Airlines. This system used two computers to connect American Airlines offices in 64 cities. In 1970, computers at four universities were connected using telephone lines to create ARPANET. The idea behind ARPANET – to allow computers in many different places to exchange information – became the basis of the Internet.

In the 1970s, computers like this one were used to send the first e-mail.

THE INTERNET

Computer researchers and scientists had long dreamt of an international network that could connect people in countries around the world. Yet until the 1980s, this was just a pipe dream.

Connection failure

There were many problems that had to be overcome before computer users around the world could easily communicate. The biggest problem during the 1970s and early 1980s was that although the number of computer networks was increasing, most of these were not connected to one another. There was no common set of rules, or protocols, and little way for people outside large universities or government agencies to use the system.

THE WORLD WIDE WEB

In 1989, a British scientist called Tim Berners-Lee created a system for sharing text and pictures over the Internet. He called this system the World Wide Web. Berners-Lee encouraged people around the world to use the World Wide Web and create their own websites. The idea caught on and today, there are nearly 1 billion websites!

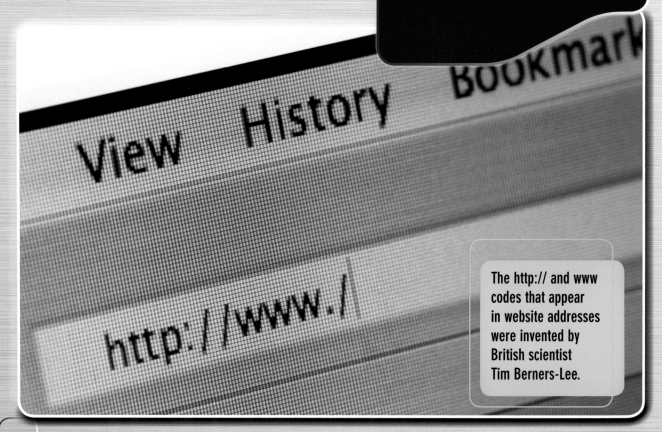

The http:// and www codes that appear in website addresses were invented by British scientist Tim Berners-Lee.

Today, computer labs are a common site at university campuses. There, students can access the Internet.

New rules

The 'international network' came a step closer in 1982. Researchers at ARPANET and DARPA (the Defense Advanced Research Projects Agency) worked together to decide on a set of rules, or protocols, for international computer networking. The system they created, which included transfer protocol (TP) and Internet protocol (IP), is still used today.

Internet for all

From the early 1990s onwards, the Internet grew rapidly. Companies called Internet service providers began to sell access to the Internet to home computer users. Anyone with a computer could join the Internet revolution. The new network age had begun.

Shopping online is possible in part thanks to the pioneering work of scientists in the 1970s and 1980s.

MOBILE NETWORKS

Thanks to wireless technology such as WiFi, today it is possible to access the Internet without using a computer. Amazingly, it is also possible to read Web pages and send e-mails using the same mobile phone network you use to make call.

Tablet computers, such as the iPad, use a combination of cellular and WiFi Internet technology.

Going mobile

The first cellular phone network was set up in the United States in 1978. It allowed people to make calls on mobile phones, which sent and received signals using radio waves to a network of masts placed around towns and cities.

Carphones

The first cellular telephones were used in the United States in 1946. They were effectively large radios and were so big that they had to be fitted inside cars. Carphones, as they became known, were of limited use and expensive but they remained in use until the 1980s.

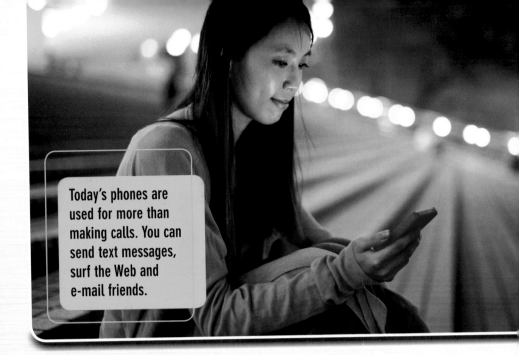

Today's phones are used for more than making calls. You can send text messages, surf the Web and e-mail friends.

Cellular network

Today's cellular network, so called because it divides the nationwide network into a series of small grids or cells, is much more advanced than the one set up in the 1970s. Each cell has its own mast and each mast is given a unique radio frequency to send and receive calls. As users pass from one cell to the next, their mobile phone will automatically detect the change and tune in to the new frequency.

WiFi boom

Smartphones, such as the iPhone, are capable not just of joining the cellular network but also of accessing the Internet using WiFi. WiFi also uses radio waves but is capable of handling much larger amounts of data than the cellular network. This makes it possible to watch live television or listen to the radio on your phone.

Early mobile phones, such as this one from the 1980s, were big, bulky and very expensive to use.

WHEN MOBILE NETWORKS FAIL

Although the cellular grid system is very stable, it can fail if it is overloaded. This happens when too many people in one cell area try to access the grid to make calls at the same time. It famously happened in New York in following the 9/11 terrorist attacks and in London after the bombings on 7 July 2005.

CHAPTER FOUR

HOW PEOPLE USE NETWORKS

The technological and scientific advances of the last 100 years have not only changed the way we communicate forever but also the way we work, study, manage our money and spend our leisure time. Without modern networks, our lives would be very different.

The Internet has revolutionised the way people discover, buy and listen to music.

USING A WEB BROWSER

Each website is stored or hosted, by an individual computer or server. The website will have its own unique address, called a URL. This enables people to search for the website online. When you type the site's address into your Web browser and press return, your computer is actually connecting to the computer or server that hosts the website.

The World Wide Web is just more than 25 years old but there are nearly 1 billion websites to surf.

Accessing information

The greatest network the world has ever seen is the World Wide Web. When we think about going on the Internet, what we usually mean is accessing the World Wide Web. It is a vast network of individual websites containing all kinds of information, resources and services. The genius of the World Wide Web is its simplicity. Using a special piece of computer software called a browser, we are able to visit any one of the websites, all in a matter of seconds.

Instant answers

Before the invention of the World Wide Web, it was much more difficult to find information. For example, today, if you want to read about the lives of the kings and queens of the British monarchy, you can find information online in seconds. Before, you would have had to go to your local library to find a book about the monarchy. Whatever you are interested in, you will find information on the Web. You can read newspaper articles, look up flight timetables, check your bank balance and find out what is showing at a local cinema. The World Wide Web puts the world at your fingertips.

SHARING INFORMATION

Today, one of our favourite pastimes is sharing things with friends online, from photos and videos to songs and important documents.

The information superhighway

Sharing online, be it uploading video clips to websites such as YouTube or putting your holiday photos on Facebook, is possible only because of the advances in network technology over recent years. In the early days of the Internet, people connected using ordinary telephone lines that were capable of carrying only small amounts of information, quite slowly. Today's fibre optic and broadband cables can transport enormous amounts of information incredibly quickly.

Force for good?

Those who use and rely on file-sharing sites believe they are a force for good. Those inside the music and film industries may not agree. Music and film executives have seen their profits fall as more people illegally swap songs and films online. The first online file-sharing service to clash with the entertainment industry was MP3-sharing service Napster.

Using your digital camera and your personal network, you can take a photo and upload it to the Internet in seconds.

Users can upload music videos using their phones, so sites like YouTube often have unauthorised videos on them.

How does a P2P network work?

Unlike regular networks, which use the 'client and host' system, storing information on dedicated servers, peer-to-peer networks do not use a dedicated server. Instead, each computer on the network acts like a mini server whose files (MP3s, movies and so on) can be accessed by all the other users on the network.

Peer-to-peer networks

Napster was one of the first file-sharing services to use a free technology called peer-to-peer (P2P) networking. Napster's cutting-edge software allowed users all over the world to download MP3 files from other users without paying for them. Today, illegal file sharing using P2P networks is as popular as ever, despite the efforts of governments to shut down these services.

Sharing photos online is simple thanks to mobile phones and wireless Internet technology.

TALKING TO THE WORLD

Not so long ago, we used landline phones and standard postal services to keep in touch with friends and family. Now, thanks to modern communications and computer networks, we can chat with the world 24 hours a day.

Hands-free devices for mobile phones, which use Bluetooth technology, allow drivers to chat with their friends while they drive.

Messages to the hub

Social networks such as Facebook, Snapchat and Twitter have revolutionised the way people keep in touch with one another. They are called social networking sites because although they are based around websites, they act like a network, connecting us with friends, family and acquaintances. If one of your 'friends' is online, you can chat by typing in short messages, like a conversation.

Video conference calls, using services such as Skype, have changed the way people keep in touch with their friends and family.

Video calls

Another great advance is video conferencing, such as Google Hangout, FaceTime or Skype. These services allow you to make video calls using your laptop, mobile phone or a computer connected to a webcam. They use a new version of old-fashioned television technology, with a little bit of Internet magic thrown in. Because they do not rely on old-fashioned telephone networks, calls cost much less than regular phone calls. In fact, video calls to other registered service users are free.

SKYPE

Using Skype, you can make calls to other Skype users for free over the Internet or a cellular network. This is made possible because Skype mixes two types of network technology: P2P networking and client-server. When you make a call, the service uses the Internet to connect you directly to the other person's computer or smartphone, rather than the telephone or cellular networks.

HAVING FUN

The network revolution brought about by fibre optic cables and the worldwide spread of the Internet has not just changed the way we keep in touch. It has also changed the way we have fun and spend our free time.

Thanks to the Internet, you can now play games against rivals on the other side of the world.

Entertainment express

The speed of modern-day fibre optic cables and their ability to carry huge amounts of data at once have made it possible to do many things online that would previously have been impossible. You can now watch high definition movies and television shows on your computer, play online games against people in different countries and watch your favourite sports teams from the comfort of your sofa.

Shopping made easy

Before the Internet age, shopping was something people had to plan into their days. They would have to go to their high street or take the bus or train into town. Today, there are so many online stores that you can shop from the comfort of your own home. Whatever you want to buy, from clothes and electrical goods to music and groceries, you can find it online and have it delivered to your door – often at cheaper prices than in local stores.

ONLINE GAMING

Online gaming is a great example of a client-server relationship. The game players are the clients. They connect over the Internet to the gaming network's server. This server responds to the instructions or requests from the players. It tracks the game, displaying the action on computers or game consoles, before you can say, 'Your turn!'

Mobile giant television screens, like this one in Poland, allow crowds to watch events, even if they are far away from the action.

KEEPING SECRETS

Not all networks can be accessed by anyone. In fact, even in this age of mass global communication, there are still many secret or closed networks that can be accessed only by a select few computer users.

Keep out!

Closed or secret networks are networks that allow access only to a limited number of people. Most are classified as secure networks, which means that they are protected by security measures such as passwords or other special computer software. Many governments use closed networks to make sensitive information, such as that used by the police or secret services, inaccessible to terrorists. However, occasionally, information from these secure networks becomes public. This is what happened when the WikiLeaks website made public thousands of secret communications between officials in different countries.

US President Obama and his advisors kept up with the hunt for Osama Bin Laden by watching live video footage beamed over a secret spy network.

The police and other emergency services used closed, secure networks to get help to people who need it.

Intranet

Not all closed networks are so secretive. Many companies, schools and universities routinely set up their own private Internet network to securely share information and resources. A private Internet site that can be accessed only by those in a specific institution is known as an intranet.

Another good example of a closed network is the system of automatic teller machines (ATMs) operated by banks for clients to withdraw and deposit cash. Although the ATMs are all connected to computer servers, for security purposes they are not connected to the Internet at large.

THE SILK ROAD

In recent years, a number of hidden networks have been created to allow anonymous Internet users the chance to buy and sell things that are illegal, such as drugs. The most famous of these networks was 'The Silk Road', an online marketplace similar to eBay. Although the FBI shut down The Silk Road, there are still many illegal networks.

NETWORK WORLD

Networks are all around us, enhancing our lives and enabling us to communicate with each other wherever we are in the world. More than ever before, we rely on them to work, study, play and keep in touch.

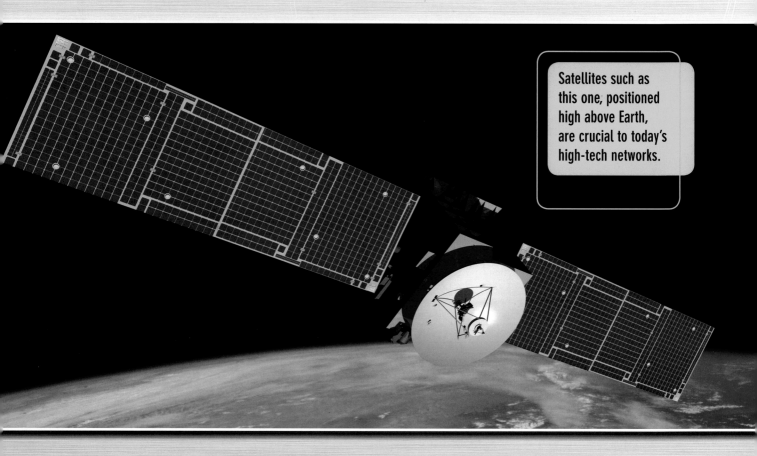

Satellites such as this one, positioned high above Earth, are crucial to today's high-tech networks.

Hidden networks

While we are aware of many of the networks we use each day, there are others that are vitally important but we may not even realise that we are using them. Most of these networks are based on cutting-edge satellites positioned high above Earth. These send and receive data via radio waves and huge transmitters on the ground. The global television news coverage we take for granted is only possible thanks to this network of space satellites. The same can be said for the Global Positioning System, the satellite network that powers car navigation systems, keeps flights on track and allows people to use apps such as GoogleMaps on their smartphones to find their way.

Security issues

As we move deeper into the twenty-first century and networks become ever more advanced, fears increase for their security. Governments spend billions every year on network security to stop criminals and terrorists stealing our money or bringing the world to its knees. So far, there have been few major disasters caused by network security failures but some experts think it will only be a matter of time before one happens. We rely so much on communications networks, such as the Internet, that we would be lost without them.

INTERNET FOR ALL

At present, nearly 40 per cent of the world has access to the Internet. By 2020, experts think the Internet will be available, in one form or another, to everyone on the planet. They also say that connection speeds will be more than 100 times faster than they are today!

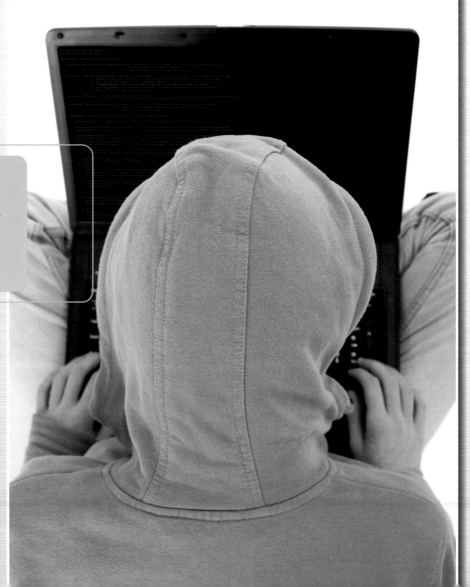

Computer hackers try to break through the security systems of modern secure networks in order to carry out crimes.

GLOSSARY

acquaintances people you know, but who are not friends or family

bluetooth a wireless system that allows mobile phones and other devices to communicate with each other

broadband an Internet connection that can transport much more information than a traditional telephone line

communication the exchange of thoughts, opinions or information

computer data information sent and received by computers or similar electronic devices

data information

download to transfer something from the Internet onto your personal computer or smartphone

Ethernet a type of cable used for connecting, or networking, computers

fibre optic cables cables made up of many long, thin strands of plastic or glass

global worldwide

Internet a network of smaller computer networks that join together to form a single global network

intranet a computer network that can be accessed only by a small number of people

millisecond one-thousandth of a second

modem a device that allows computers to send and receive information over the telephone network

protocols rules

radio waves invisible waves of energy that can pass through the air

revolutionised dramatically changed

satellite a device sent into space for a specific purpose, for example, enabling communication

server a super-computer designed for a specific task, for example, storing information or running a network

software a computer application or program designed to do a specific task, for example, sending e-mail, editing photos or recording music

transmit to send information

transmitter a device that transmits or sends, information, often in the form of radio waves or electrical signals

upload to transfer something from your computer to a website or Internet server

USB short for Universal Serial Bus: a system for connecting electronic equipment to a computer

webcam a small video camera that connects to your computer and allows you to send and receive video messages or record videos on your computer

website a collection of writing, pictures, music and sound that is stored on a computer and made available to everyone on the World Wide Web

WiFi a system that allows computers and mobile phones to connect to computer networks without a traditional system of cables

wireless technology that allows the exchange of information, but does not require wires

World Wide Web the global network of websites

FOR MORE INFORMATION

Books

Grayson, Robert. *Careers in Network Engineering*. Rosen Classroom, 2011.

Greve, Meg. *How it Works: The Internet*. Rourke Educational Media, 2014.

Martin, Claudia. *Inspirational Lives: Tim Berners-Lee*. Wayland, 2015.

Websites

Find out how mobile phones work at:
www.ehow.com/how-does_4564386_cell-phones-work.html

For more information on how the Internet works, log on at:
www.internetsociety.org/internet/how-it-works

Find out more about Internet infrastructures at:
http://computer.howstuffworks.com/internet/basics/ internet-infrastructure.htm

INDEX